MESA
BLANCA

MESA BLANCA

WHITE ALTAR

FLORENCIO GUEVARA

Mesa Blanca

Copyright © 2019 by Florencio Guevara. All rights reserved.

No part of this publication may be reproduced, stored in a retrieval system or transmitted in any way by any means, electronic, mechanical, photocopy, recording or otherwise without the prior permission of the author except as provided by USA copyright law.

The opinions expressed by the author are not necessarily those of URLink Print and Media.

1603 Capitol Ave., Suite 310 Cheyenne, Wyoming USA 82001
1-888-980-6523 | admin@urlinkpublishing.com

URLink Print and Media is committed to excellence in the publishing industry.

Book design copyright © 2019 by URLink Print and Media. All rights reserved.

Published in the United States of America

Library of Congress Control Number: 2019918784
ISBN 978-1-64367-994-5 (Paperback)
ISBN 978-1-64367-993-8 (Digital)

18.07.19

CONTENTS

The Battlefield 9
Preparing for a Mesa Blanca 11
The Prayers 14
The Arrival of the Quadrants 16
The Misa Continues 20
The Aftermath 24
Let's Get Ready to Rumble…! 25
Trinkets and Beads 28
Opening the Gates 30
Some Examples of Spirits Working 35
Correct Mediumnistic Actions 37
Team Work, Not Competition 39
Tidbits to Remember . . . and Forget! 43
Pennies, Pesos, and Piggy Banks… 49
Recipes from the Quadrant's Pantry 52
Tomorrow's News Tonight..62
The Dangers of Translations...65
Thoughts and Prayers..68
Demons and Devices...82

DEDICATION

For my wife, Elvia, without whom my life would have continued to be as empty as the day before I met her. Our souls are one. Blessed be . . .

THE BATTLEFIELD

When but a small child, I remember seeing a large group of people sitting around a long table. A most distinguishing feature of this table was the clean, white linen cloth that covered it at every meeting. It reached halfway down to the floor. Atop the table, centered, were usually a standing crucifix and at least one vessel of water. These were usually the flat, round goldfish bowls, half filled with tap water. And, of course, either a household white candle, or a large, glass-encased seven-day devotional.

Imprinted forever on my soul are the scenes and sounds of those meetings. In good Puerto Rican Spanish, they are known as "sesiones". Among other Hispanic groups they could be known as a "misa", "reunion", or "trabajo". Whatever title they chose, all are in agreement that the root word for this type of séance is "Mesa Blanca". It literally translates as "the White Table". To this day, it is the pinnacle of mediumnistic development and a battlefield between good and evil! Whereas the earlier Anglo mediums used their gift only as a proof of communication from the other side, in the Spanish-speaking world the Mesa Blanca was a tool for healing, un-hexing, divinatory teaching, and helping individuals set their daily lives in order. So, too, the spirits who were summoned to these tables were given the opportunity to mend fences with those they harmed in any way, as well as further their growth and development toward the light of the spiritual schooling offered by the mediums' guardian spirits.

Few, if any, in Puerto Rico, were concerned about the now famous table rapping, smoky ghost plasma, metal bending, or spook hunting. The prized purpose of any Mesa Blanca was the direct spirit communication that would enable the mediums to help those attending. In addition to the messages from across the veil, everyone awaits instructions, hands-on intervention, and guidance on how best to conduct themselves in life. Some come for business decisions, while others come in search of health and social situations.

However, the people to really watch in any misa are those that attend because they suspect "dark spirits" are causing suffering in their lives. These concerns can come from various levels of attack. There are spirits that are simply looking for the person's attention because they have a calling to take part in the Great Work. This person is usually a medium who is beginning to understand their power. Spiritists know that when God sends a medium into this world, that person cannot avoid the responsibility of assisting their spirits to partake in the Great Work. To refuse is to invite a life of tribulations and illnesses for which most doctors will find scant relief. Prospective mediums know why they would be suffering.

Too often we in the spiritual circles mistakenly believe that everyone has an "antenna" to the other side. Since we tend to seek each other out, we forget that mediums are a lighthouse. Within the ocean of darkness on this planet we are the beams that illuminate humanity with understanding. The vast majority of people are not mediums. Indeed, during an emergency God can use anyone as a medium. Usually, though, people are led to a medium for direction and purpose.

Mesa Blanca is a tool that forges an alliance between brain and spirit for the integration of the spirit guides in a cohesive manner that our everyday lives may proceed without too many conflicts.

Every misa has three stages of action. Steps cannot be skipped or abbreviated. Preparations for a misa are equally important.

THE BATTLEFIELD

When but a small child, I remember seeing a large group of people sitting around a long table. A most distinguishing feature of this table was the clean, white linen cloth that covered it at every meeting. It reached halfway down to the floor. Atop the table, centered, were usually a standing crucifix and at least one vessel of water. These were usually the flat, round goldfish bowls, half filled with tap water. And, of course, either a household white candle, or a large, glass-encased seven-day devotional.

Imprinted forever on my soul are the scenes and sounds of those meetings. In good Puerto Rican Spanish, they are known as "sesiones". Among other Hispanic groups they could be known as a "misa", "reunion", or "trabajo". Whatever title they chose, all are in agreement that the root word for this type of séance is "Mesa Blanca". It literally translates as "the White Table". To this day, it is the pinnacle of mediumnistic development and a battlefield between good and evil! Whereas the earlier Anglo mediums used their gift only as a proof of communication from the other side, in the Spanish-speaking world the Mesa Blanca was a tool for healing, un-hexing, divinatory teaching, and helping individuals set their daily lives in order. So, too, the spirits who were summoned to these tables were given the opportunity to mend fences with those they harmed in any way, as well as further their growth and development toward the light of the spiritual schooling offered by the mediums' guardian spirits.

Few, if any, in Puerto Rico, were concerned about the now famous table rapping, smoky ghost plasma, metal bending, or spook hunting. The prized purpose of any Mesa Blanca was the direct spirit communication that would enable the mediums to help those attending. In addition to the messages from across the veil, everyone awaits instructions, hands-on intervention, and guidance on how best to conduct themselves in life. Some come for business decisions, while others come in search of health and social situations.

However, the people to really watch in any misa are those that attend because they suspect "dark spirits" are causing suffering in their lives. These concerns can come from various levels of attack. There are spirits that are simply looking for the person's attention because they have a calling to take part in the Great Work. This person is usually a medium who is beginning to understand their power. Spiritists know that when God sends a medium into this world, that person cannot avoid the responsibility of assisting their spirits to partake in the Great Work. To refuse is to invite a life of tribulations and illnesses for which most doctors will find scant relief. Prospective mediums know why they would be suffering.

Too often we in the spiritual circles mistakenly believe that everyone has an "antenna" to the other side. Since we tend to seek each other out, we forget that mediums are a lighthouse. Within the ocean of darkness on this planet we are the beams that illuminate humanity with understanding. The vast majority of people are not mediums. Indeed, during an emergency God can use anyone as a medium. Usually, though, people are led to a medium for direction and purpose.

Mesa Blanca is a tool that forges an alliance between brain and spirit for the integration of the spirit guides in a cohesive manner that our everyday lives may proceed without too many conflicts.

Every misa has three stages of action. Steps cannot be skipped or abbreviated. Preparations for a misa are equally important.

PREPARING FOR A MESA BLANCA

Today's mediums often stray from the norm when setting the table for the séance or the traditional misa. It can be a matter of taste, or of their spiritual quadrant's preference, just as long as it doesn't pass into the realm of being so flashy that the layout takes attention away from the focus that should be directed toward the table during the Working.

There is a simple setup that has been used throughout these centuries. It consists of the bowl or glass of water, the candle, the crucifix, and flowers, usually white, atop a table cloth of white cotton fabric. I jokingly refer to this setup as old school spiritism. You can, though, have other things present on the table. There can be a statue of the Christ as the centerpiece. Alongside this statue you may have one of the advocations of the Virgin Mary, or of any other saint. During special misas for the dead it is not uncommon to see photographs of the deceased next to the crucifix. It will serve as a point of reference during the misa for the deceased.

Some people like to have an abundance of flowers, and others enjoy putting herbs in water. These herbs will serve as cleansing tools either when the mediums need them, or at the end of the Mesa Blanca to bless all who attend.

There should not be many candles on the table. One is fine, but two can be used to signify the spiritual and material planes of life. This makes better sense when we realize that everyday problems are dealt with in a séance, just as much as situations on a spirit level. When lighting the two candles, if you're facing the table, be sure to illuminate the left one first. Left represents spirit, right material.

However, you will find that the great majority of mediums will insist on the traditionalist method of having only one flame on the altar. The flame of a candle is a major point of concentration and a homing beam for souls from the abyss. It serves as a filter for entities to line up and come through in an orderly manner. Plain household white candles are best. Have plenty on hand. A glass cylinder, seven-day candle may also be used. This cancels the repetitive lighting of candles, avoiding their burning out and interrupting throughout the misa. If these are used, I highly suggest that they be put into clear, glass vases that are filled with water at least one-third.

Another item that is a staple of any séance is the cleansing solution that is prepared and blessed by the medium setting up the altar. This consists of a rather large bowl or pail of water. To this the medium, while praying for blessings and radiating the water with the spirits' vibrations, will add petals from one or more flowers. Discard the stem and buds. To this the medium will pour in small amounts of holy water, Florida water, and perhaps one or more perfumed waters to provide all those attending with protection and preparation before and after the Mesa Blanca. When the prayers begin, everyone, in a clockwise formation, will come up to the altar and dip their hands into this solution, give themselves the "passes", and then sit again to re-join the prayers in progress. The only break in this comes if there are any children or pregnant ladies at the misa. The children go before all in chronological order, youngest to oldest, and then any pregnant woman. Then the rest, in clockwise order of seating.

If the traditionalist form is being used, with the mediums sitting around the table, the table must be simply set, so all can view each other across the table and behind the mediums to where the others are seated. If the more modern altar type of table is set, up against a wall, then the seating is different. Here there will be two chairs at either end of the table, facing the "audience". These are referred to as "point" or "punta". They are occupied by the chair and co-chair of mediums running the reunion. The people who occupy these positions should be experienced mediums, as they will be the first receiving targets of the vibrations that hit upon the table. The others will face the table in a semi-circle. Gender does not play a role in presiding a misa. Indeed, more women than men are found sitting at point.

I prefer this layout because it provides a strong focal point for the mediums. In the open space the subject in question is visible to all and the concentration is strongest. When any medium is physically working with the subject, the attention and prayers of all are much more direct.

THE PRAYERS

The first step is by far the most important to any misa. Prayer is humanity's strongest weapon, and the one it uses the least. It cannot be seen or felt, but its results are historically proven to work, no matter what religion or cultural environment you find yourself in. For the Mesa Blanca, the book that is the most widely used in the world is the Collection of Devotional Prayers by Allan Kardec, the father of modern spiritism. Mr. Kardec's prayer book is used in many languages. Unfortunately, the English translation is completely botched up. An attempt was made by some anonymous fool to translate literally. Literally, nothing can be translated. It is the essence of the idea that is translated, taking account cultural definitions. I have tried unsuccessfully to communicate with the publishers to bring their attention to this glaring problem. One day, hopefully, the publishers will get it right!

The first prayer from the book is the opening of the reunion. This is followed by the prayers for the mediums, guardian angels, those beloved departed, and peace in the home. Additionally, there are poems that were dictated by mediums in France that are prayers. As the prayers continue, the quadrants begin to align themselves with their respective mediums. They begin providing insight to the mediums for the work ahead with visions and inspirations mentally as the prayers progress. During this time special prayers, such as health and childbirth assistance, can be requested.

One word of caution to all mediums regarding this first step in a misa. Never attempt to abbreviate this time in the séance. By whittling away at the time spent on prayer, you are removing parts of the umbrella of protection from above. Prayers are the main source of nourishment for the spirits. Their strength will maintain the dark entities at bay and keep their mischief from stunting a misa. You have been warned…!

THE ARRIVAL OF THE QUADRANTS

At this time, the medium chairing the misa will ask the mediums to begin passing through their quadrants. Usually, as a long-time warrior of the misas, I will pass one or two of my spirit guides to very briefly clean me. It is never good to have the spirits prolong their stay while opening up the medium at this stage. Time must be given so all the mediums that can pass their quadrants have the same opportunity to do so. Then, after this short step, the séance is officially under way.

The chair will ask for anyone having visions for the misa's impending work to speak. Here, the person will always say, "With the 'table's' permission, " and then state what they saw as the prayers began. When all who have seen have spoken, then it will become obvious to all that the time for the Great Work has begun.

As this third step of the misa begins, the chair or the co-chair will be inspired to call a particular subject to stand and come to the center. Here the mediums, especially any who have had a vision with them during the prayers, will begin to describe what they pick up on the subject. Some questions may be asked to clear any gray areas in the visions. As the mediums continue to pick up on this particular subject, the chair will notice the medium that is receiving the brunt of the "jolts" and vibrations associated with this case. Special attention will be given to this medium. The experience of the two "point" chairs now comes into play.

If they know that the medium is a trance medium capable of picking up a negative entity, one of them will be ready to be the sole interrogator. It is important to remember that all other questions be transferred through the point.

This way there is a filter during this lifting of the dark spirit with a minimum of danger to the working medium. To allow helter-skelter questions and comments from many people at once is to weaken the safety net of the medium's quadrant and risk the entity's escape from the quadrant.

As the interrogation proceeds, the chair will instruct the entity to lift all the negativity it has wrought on the subject. A vessel of water for collecting that had been set up prior will be put in front of the medium holding the spirit. By lifting both hands and picking up from the aura, the spirit will lift and deposit into the waters the witchcraft and vibrations that are on the subject. At no time will the medium's hands actually enter the water. Rather the hands will thump on the lip of the vessel, so that the palms of the medium release the vibrational rays towards the water. This will be done over and over again until the interrogator is satisfied that all the "crud" has been lifted from the subject.

At that point, the spirit will be asked to plead forgiveness from the subject. The spirit will then be ready to declare that the Lord's peace be with all. Once that happens, the interrogator must forcefully instruct this spirit on following those spirits of the medium's quadrant that are holding it and getting ready to transport the entity to the spiritual "colleges" where it will find healing and be given penance in the form of future help in order to cleanse itself and balance the Akashic record.

"Dear spirit," the voice of the interrogator. "Follow the instructions of those spirits of light. They will be leading you to a much better place where you will find peace for your soul and be able to grow. Someday you will be in light and free.

Then you will be returning to perform as a positive force and undo all the accumulated damage you have done to others as well as yourself. Now leave the medium without disturbing the quadrant! In the name of God, bless you and safe passage!"

Immediately as the spirit leaves through the medium's passes, the call goes out to the quadrant. "Oh guardian angel, come to the aid and restoration of your medium. Clean them well of all impurities. Then take three steps back…"

Once the medium's guardian has cleaned them and spoken a holy greeting, the medium will then come out of the trance. Usually, the chair calls for the Lord's Prayer out loud by all, and the Hail Mary, and Glory Be To God prayers, as well. Once that has been done, the subject should be sat down again and we can move on to the next case that vibrationally the chairs pick up.

During this time, there should have been a concentrated silence among all at the misa. Picking up a dark spirit is a rather dangerous task for any medium. The risks involved from a lack of concentration and prayer can involve the incomplete cleaning of the subject, therefore the medium can be left with many impurities afterward. This will necessitate for the medium to have to be cleansed by another to avoid suffering from the subject's negativities.

Another probability due to the lack of discipline in a Mesa Blanca, is that the medium will wind up taking the dark entity home if no one is alert. Spirits will try to wrangle out of giving up their evil, especially if they were sent by an enemy of the subject. If the interrogators cannot concentrate and the prayers are not being said to help in the workings of the medium, then this danger is quite real.

I have attended misas where people were allowed to talk and comment during the time a medium is possessed. Sometimes, three and four mediums were passing spirits and giving out messages while one was breaking a hex! That is madness… It contributes to half-baked solutions for those attending, and opens the doors to mischief.

It is a crying shame that the control in these misas was naught! What were the chairs thinking? Were they qualified to be at point? Weren't they instrtucted on the safety issues for the mediums as well as those in attendance?

In my lifetime of mediumship, rarrely have I seen anyone with enough power to allow simultaneous possessions to proceed successfully. Most misas are held in a person's home, usually the dining room or the garage, if it's cool enough. There is no reason for a small gathering of people not to concentrate and provide proper protection to mediums that put their sanity on the line for others. Remember the sanctity of the home is also at stake. You do not want the wrong vibes left in your house because no one was really controlling effectively.

The result of good control is a misa that will leave the host's home blessed and all that attended feeling better about themselves and what was achieved by the mediums. Word of mouth is the one big calling card in this field. Personal recommendations, rather than commercial advertising, are what enhances a medium's reputation. In all cultures this is a fact of life, but among Hispanics, bilingual or not, especially so.

THE MISA CONTINUES . . .

Once all have settled down after working on that first case, either the chairs will call on the next person whose vibrations are "hitting on the table" or another medium will ask to speak and state a vision about another member of the group. In all this, it is important to remember that the mediums aren't the only ones that can give visions. In attendance will be persons who are in the beginning stages of developing their mediumship. These individuals should verbally be encouraged during the Mesa Blanca to talk about any vision or feeling they get as this could be instrumental in helping a subject. Even those who are not mediums need to feel comfortable in this regard. Many folks feel shy about speaking up during a misa. They may feel embarrassed if they say something that may not make sense to them. Being in a group where there are sharp mediums will probably make anyone feel vulnerable to ridicule.

An explanation of how visions are acquired will help ease any misgivings a person may have toward speaking up. Everyone is born with a guardian angel. At any given time this spirit may provide you with a vision or inspiration if it is necessary at any given time. If, for any reason, the mediums have not picked up on a specific detail or person in the group, then the average person will have their "antenna" opened up.

The vast majority of people are not mediums, even though God can employ any person as a vehicle at any given time. Mediums are lighthouses in the dark, illuminating the world on the other side of the veil. As such we will attract many spirits to us. We are born with a quadrant of spirits assigned to us along with our Guardian of the Gate---our guardian angel. This spirit's function is to open the door for any of our spirits to come through and partake in the Great Work (La Obra). In this way, these spirits will be able to complete the tasks they have been assigned as well as balance out their ledger with the Light.

Of course, it goes without saying that there will also be negative and stray spirits attracted to our beam. In this rather cruel world many a soul has met their demise in violence or abject solitude. Some have never even been remembered by loved ones. It is these spirits that the mediums have to deal with constantly.

But, the act of providing a conduit to redemption has its compensations in spite of the trouble they cause us. More than half of my quadrant is made up of spirits I lifted in misas as negative or evil entities. Once they were enlightened in the spiritual colleges across the veil, which can take years or decades, they have opted to return to my quadrant to help me as a way of thanking my quadrant.

However, let's return to the misa.

In between the cases that are worked, or after every two, the chair should pass around Agua Florida or whatever spiritual cologne is being used. With this small amount poured into their palms, everyone will give themselves the passes to cleanse and re-energize their auras. In particular if the preceding case involved heavy emotions and currents, it is in the best interest of all to have this done.

As the misa proceeds on to the other cases, the chairs should keep an occasional eye on the clock. Why? Among the reasons, foremost is fatigue. You do not want your mediums burned out. It is quite draining of the energy source when working a misa and dealing with the onslaught of emotions from people.

Another powerful reason is the fact that after midnight, you really are courting negativity with all those tired people. After all, they've been sitting there since approximately seven in the evening, which is traditionally the start of misas.

By eleven forty-five, the Mesa Blanca should begin to wrap up. The chair will ask whether all feel normal, checking that no one is feeling spiritually ill. If so, this person will be given a quick cleaning by one or more mediums. Then, without further ado, the chair will ask all to stand for the closing prayer. This prayer is found in the Coleccion or it can be voiced out loud in a simple thanks for God and all the angelic oversouls as well as quadrants who provided help during this misa. And with that, the misa closes.

Once this occurs, most turn off the candles, while others keep them going until they finish burning. It depends on whether they are the glass-encased devotionals, put in some water, or the household candles. The solution for cleansing is to be thrown out. Usually, a son or daughter of Yemaya will be asked to take the bowl or pail out to the street, and dump it towards the middle of the road. Often the chair does it. The vessel of water that was used to collect negative vibes is emptied into the toilet or dumped into the ground. The earth holds all, its core burning off all evil. The rest of the table can either be left for the host to clean the next morning, or all the waters can be emptied at that time.

Any herbs or flowers that are on the floor that were used to clean with, should be disposed of in an outdoor garbage can. The floor should be swept or mopped, depending on the home. When one is celebrating a Mesa Blanca at a home one does not inhabit, it is wise to help the host or hostess be left with an area that was exactly as it was before the misa.

Once that is complete, then the host or hostess should have prepared snacks and refreshments. After a misa, the body definitely needs fuel! This could consist of sandwiches, cookies, cake, coffee, and soft drinks. Some of us in the Hispanic community might even serve rice, beans, and meat! Even others will make a tasty lasagna….

Yummy…It all comes down to the personal tastes of the crowd. I will say this much, good "café con leche" or espresso will be an absolute staple for me!

A word of caution here. Many diabetics can be found in a misa. The host/hostess should have coffee on the warmer or cookies or refreshments at the ready in case someone's sugar plummets. Please ask at the onset of the misa if there are diabetics in the group. They will be forever grateful.

THE AFTERMATH

Once the people have eaten, some may stay a bit and converse, while others will go home. For those that stay, word of caution. Watch what is commented on after a misa. I have a self-imposed rule on my conversation after a misa: anything but the misa!

I hate continuing the misa in public conversations. Incidents, information, and misunderstandings can occur in any misa. It is very important that everyone just chill out after any Mesa Blanca and enjoy the food, as well as the company. What happens in a séance, stays there. If you need to copy a prescription by the spirits or wanted to question a medium about an entity, you should have done it while the séance was in session.

When I am hosting any misa, I make it my business to let the guests know that I don't want them engaging in misa-related conversations. This is territory ripe with problematic topics that can rile anyone. It can bring into play personality clashes as well as opening the door to some holier than though person to comment on how <u>they</u> would have handled things. This is akin to Monday morning quarterbacking---and totally unwanted at a moment of relaxation. To this type of tension builder I say: go on a mattress for your own tension!

Ending a misa in as much peace and fun conversation is just as important as any other step in the Mesa Blanca. Laughter…the elixir of the soul.

LET'S GET READY TO RUMBLE…!

Mediums are like anyone else, with their distinct personalities, likes and dislikes. Culturally, they are products of their upbringing and this imprint leaves a definite point of view toward the world. Any medium needs to read extensively. Material concerning spiritual matters will definitely occupy the larger portion of the list of books, articles, and media. Getting to know about other world cultures is just as important, however. In this part of the world, that means comprehending the cultures of North and South America. The Caribbean and Central America are geographically associated with North America. The isthmus of Panama is the connecting waistline between the American continents.

During a misa there will be various points of view that are rooted in cultural upbringing. One person, for instance, may view a wayward spirit as an entity to be managed through incense, kind words and prayer. Another may be convinced that this entity needs to be lifted and sent to the spiritual "schools of light" in order to find their true path and objective within the sphere of the positive. There could even be a third person who views the spirit as an arrival to the subject's quadrant.

Here is where these differences of opinion are filtered through the sieve provided by the chairpersons and the elder mediums of the group. After conversing about how the spirit is being felt in the misa's environment, the medium that is receiving the actual vibrations from that entity will be allowed to pass this entity through and into the midst of the Mesa Blanca. It will then be allowed to speak and be interrogated by one delegated person who will field any questions from the group. Remember only one interrogator.

Once this has taken place successfully, the spirit will be instructed and given prayer to be on their way. They will be escorted by the other spirits of the medium's quadrant. Afterwards, of course, the medium will have the guardian that was "holding" this visiting spirit clean them and their aura.

All this should have answered the various viewpoints of the others, mediums or not. The chairperson(s) should avoid any further comments that could lead to a prolonged disagreement and tinge the atmosphere with tension. We are gathered to work in unison, not division.

Which brings me to the big worry that I always experience during all séances: the ego trips, the Messiah complex, and the "my 'culito' don't stink attitude! Share that chuckle with your Hispanic friend…

The holier-than-thou characters unfortunately dot the spiritual landscape in great numbers. Fortunately for the world, these individuals never unite due to their enduring conflicts with just about anyone who doesn't see it their way---especially each other! God help us if they ever united on any single issue. It would resemble a tsunami of gremlins upon us…

Mediums need to be flexible enough to investigate and question before they pass judgment on any psychic event. Different eyes see things from a varying slant. One opinion alone cannot be the sole tool for working with an entity or vision. All opinions need to be investigated during the misa, without anyone uttering disparaging remarks that belittle the other mediums' skills. If someone doesn't comprehend what a speaker means at a misa, it is best to ask for clarification, rather than explode with indignation. Count to ten if necessary.

Losing one's temper can cause many distasteful incidents in a séance. The chair must intervene with words that both soothe and allow for both views to be looked into before a decision or judgment is taken. If the chairperson doesn't have the skill at mediating between two mediums that insist on their point of view, then get ready for a bit of a boxing match... or worse! Yes, there have been misas that have ended in a melee, believe it or not... It's quite sad for the person being worked on at the time, because of the vibrational interruption that could cause continued suffering. But, trust me, is it ever going to be fodder for the fools who adore the gossip hot line!

All of us who've been in this field for an extensive period of time know all too well the role of gossip among mediums. Prestige and credibility suffer because of it. The cardinal rule: what is said in a misa, stays in a misa.

You may receive various calls from persons that are curious as to what happened in a misa that they did not attend. Likewise, another might call to procure you point of view about any part of the séance---and a second after you hang up, will call others with a distorted answer that will cause the misinformation to grow into a cancerous gossip capable of ruining many friendships.

Remember that misas often deal with subjects that are delicate and private. Respect for the subjects attended during the Work is best shown by silence. Remember the Golden Rule ...

TRINKETS AND BEADS . . .

You may wonder what to wear to a séance. In today's atmosphere, one doesn't want to be an attention-hound for the wrong reasons. Clothing and accessories can make you opaque. Make the mediums' antennas target your aura, not your flashy apparel.

When it comes to the actual outfit, subtlety is the norm. Most people attend misas dressed in white from head to toe. This is your best option. It is not just the color of purity, rather it provides a neutral backdrop that will enable the mediums to see even clearer through your spiritual situation. Having several white outfits will be helpful, particularly when there will be moments that leave them less than white! We'll talk about that in a bit.

Women should shy away from wearing pants or shorts to these reunions. Always consult with the host if it is their policy that the ladies wear skirts. Most of the time, the answer will be positive. The skirt or dress should be loose, comfortable, and definitely *not* a miniskirt. If the host approves of pants, please make sure that's indeed what they are! Too many people today confuse leggings with pants. Trust me---it will not be appreciated to show up wrapped in a second tight skin with nothing left to the imagination. Most places will give you a spare skirt or ask you to go home and change!

Jewelry is fine. Indeed many mediums and spiritual beings, male or female, possess jewelry that is of a religious nature. Gold and silver bracelets as well as medals are quite commonly worn. A conservative taste is best.

Continuing with jewelry, there are specific necklaces that are part of the African religious roots. Santeria, Palo Mayombe, Sanses (21 Divisions), Voudou, Obiya, among others, have specific uses for the beads. Often in necklace form, they often are used as ankle bracelets, wrist bracelets, or strewn across shoulder and chest. The chairperson of any Mesa Blanca must announce that all who are wearing these "tools" *must* remove them and put them in their pockets or purses.

What must be remembered at all times is that the beads themselves are not the sacred part of the necklace. The actual #10 cotton string is what is really important because it is the string itself that "eats" from the sacrificial bowls, whether animal blood or plant fluids.

As these are done to honor and identify specific entities, by not wearing the beads the subject avoids confusion and conflict between these and the spirits of the person's quadrant. You can cause a "cruce" or knotted derailment between the quadrant you're born with and the entities "placed" on your head, which are removed when you pass through the veil into the spirit realm.

The above is a situation that must not be overlooked. The mental, emotional, and spiritual health of all attending the misa is at stake!

Moving on to the male wardrobe, no sleeveless t-shirts, shorts, or hanging, low-rider pants. Make sure when you bend or squat for various cleansings that you don't "moon" the audience.

Both women and men might want to cover their heads. Women might want to wear white kerchiefs. Men might want to wear a bring beret or close to it. The religious issue should be what causes this to be a part of an outfit for a séance.

OPENING THE GATES

Passing a spirit through one's "head" is more technical than anyone can ever imagine. When I take on spiritual godchildren---the term used when an arrangement has been reached to take on a student-teacher relationship---the first thing I stress is that the success of channeling a spirit is based on a 50-50 effort. Too often inexperienced mediums tell me that they've been waiting for months or even years to feel the spirit spark up.

Trust me. Waiting for the entities to magically "poof" their way through your aura will find you still sitting there well after retirement age…! The ability to be a medium is as new to the novice as it is to the spirit that is called to work in the quadrant it's been assigned to by the Keeper of the Akashic Records.

As we begin our training session, the godchild and I begin with prayers. This will include the Lord's Prayer, Hail Mary, Glory Be…, and the several choice invocations found in Allan Kardec's <u>Collection of Devotional Prayers</u>. The prayers for the mediums, guardian spirits, at the beginning of sessions, etc., will also be read aloud.

Should the devotional not be available, direct prayer to God to help in this training session is just as good. Mediums have a natural bridge of light connecting to the other side of the veil. The mere thought of the otherworldly plane is like a shaft of light penetrating the consciousness.

"When you feel the chills or the presence of the spirit, raise your hands and fan them behind your neck in the direction of wrapping the spirit onto you. Your hands should move in a circular motion backward," I urge.

By this time the energy in the room should be quite palpable. The person is told to speed up the circular motion near the back of their head and neck on each side.

"Now, when you feel the entity fully on you, say the words for them. 'May the peace of the Lord be here.' Or 'Blessings…'." With some effort most people will mouth or outright utter the greetings. At this time, I put my hands on their shoulders and mentally instruct the spirit to take "three paces back" and stand at the ready of their medium.

"You may open your eyes now. Tell me whatever you saw, felt, heard, smelled, or even tasted."

Now the conversation moves toward the level and intensity of reception during this session. Being an extremely new medium, the person might experience very little. Indeed, some only feel the chills and the presence. But this is the beginning. The spirit is learning how to use the medium's body as a tool to communicate. As time elapses the entity will feel much more at ease in communicating through the person. The spiritualist, also, will feel much less tense when the spirit is about to come through.

These sessions will, of course, be lasting a bit longer each time, as the process of mediumship continues. The most important thing to remember is that there is no known time frame per spirit for bringing through your quadrant of entities. Every spirit is like another world. The process of assimilating the spirit's cultural background is an arduous one indeed. It's always better to read about their origins.

As you get to know your spirits, you will be drawn to them in ways you thought were reserved for the living. Over the years, the more you work with them, the more you appreciate their personalities, their likes and dislikes, as well as view matters in a way similar to them. They will have a direct influence on your life, from food to home décor.

Here is where the novice can get in trouble. It is one thing to be influenced by your spirits, and quite another for you to "materialize" them through your eyes.

The biggest culprit can be any Gypsy entity. Regardless of how romantic their life may seem to have been, Gypsies suffered and continue to suffer, ever so much. The bigotry they experience from white Europeans is extensive. In other areas of the world they are shunned. The jobs as blacksmiths, horse attendants, or carpenters have dried up for them. Even the fortune-telling by the women has left little inroads into Gypsy economics. This has opened the door to a survival of the fittest philosophy.

Many people make the mistake of providing too much materialization to Gypsy spirits. They often provide an altar complete with dolls, jewelry, and amulets that they often wear themselves on specific occasions. The result is that rather than lift up the entity into light, they ground it on the material plane where the entity will often impose their vibrations on the person and influence them directly to live as the Gypsies do. Things could really lose control here! The entity's desire to live the nomadic existence could force the person to do things that are calculated to leave them homeless, lose interest in their careers, and be flippant towards money. If anyone thinks it can't happen to them, keep materializing Gypsy souls!

When you find yourself in the crisis I did, you'll remember the warning. Keep these entities in prayer and give them nothing but an occasional candle or flower to enhance their progress toward development and light. The least material things they have to "grasp" the better.

Remember, no other spirit in the world can mesmerize you into living through their eyes like a Gypsy. With that said, we can now move on to the positive force that Gypsies represent in the medium's arsenal.

Gypsy women, as they did when alive, are the only ones that, as spirits, help a medium read for people and provide a look into the future. They may be well versed in the Tarot, or palmistry. If so, the medium will feel the calling towards any one of these or both. The medium will have to read and study intensely these systems. The Gypsies will inspire you to learn and perfect these skills.

The male Gypsies provide quite another, more personal form of protection. The tribal head of all clans is referred to as a Chief. This type of spirit imparts leadership skills to his medium. Protection from evil and provider of justice are also part of their gifts.

It is important to have a picture or statue of the Gypsy patron saint, St. Sara la Kali. Enshrined in the southwestern French coast, each May 24th and 25th she is celebrated. She is brought out down the river into the sea and back into the shrine again. You can look into the websites for her image and history. Appealing in your prayers for spiritual light will help your entities lift their existence from the earthly to the highly spiritual plane.

Any type of spiritual entity can dominate you in a material way. It's up to the medium to be responsible and caring for their quadrant. Keeping up a daily prayer ritual for up to about 15 minutes can make all the difference in the world. In addition, sit with the elder who is helping you to develop and hold a "mini" séance that is more like a classroom for your quadrant. Questions, doubts, and positive progress should all be part of this training. Since its one-on-one there is plenty of opportunity for extensive growth and contribution to the medium's self confidence. It's a good balance to the training in groups, and in the séances themselves.

Getting back to the actual passing of the spirit, once it's on you, in seconds, you will experience the following. First, thoughts will come into your head that aren't yours. Second, you will feel the need to speak about what you are feeling. And third, all of this occurs within seconds.

It's quite a lot to absorb in that micro time frame. One has to analyze what the message is by "seeing" what the spirit sees. Once that's done, effort must be exerted to provide the mouthpiece for the entity to speak. Little by little, once you are pushing your training, you will arrive at the stage where they will utter the greetings. With further time, messages will be spoken. Eventually, the medium will have achieved a degree of confidence with the spirit that they can tell just what the spirit wants to say and do.

Experience this in person with your elder. You will never forget the initial experiences that helped open the gate.

SOME EXAMPLES OF SPIRITS WORKING

There are as many types of spirits as there are cultures in existence. Time is also an intricate part in the fabric of spiritual work. Reincarnation plays an all too important role here. Often spirits are seeking contact with the souls of people who have been their parents, children, siblings, friends, lovers, or enemies in past lives. The relationship will determine, of course, how to proceed with the contact.

One of the main "work horses" of the Mesa Blanca is a spirit we lovingly refer to as a "madama". These are usually souls of African or mulatto women that carry the brunt of the Great Work. Among Latins, these entities are looked upon as motherly, good luck angels. It is often necessary to explain to Afro-Americans why this "mammy" figure is not a denigration of black women. In the U.S., this figure was culturally seen as a negative reminder of slavery. Not so in the Hispanic world. The stark, hateful slavery of the U.S. was not the norm. In Latin America slavery was not as dead-ended as thought. Slaves were often treated well, many were emancipated early, and there was much interracial marriage. Hence, the mulattos, the olive-skinned, and the abundance of families with children that could range from brown to white.

The madamas were seen as caretakers, nannies, cooks, and providers of most of the nurturing in any household. This carried on into the spirit world. These spirits are all too often quite motherly and loving with those they protect. During séances it is common to see them spearheading the lifting of evil spirits. They are masters when it comes to cleansing auras and prescribing herbs, foods, prayers, and mixtures for healing.

Word of caution, though. They can sometimes be quite entertaining through the use of rather colorful language. It is very important for any medium that has them in their quadrant to educate and lift them through prayer. Madamas are known for their brutal honesty, interlaced with a sarcastic joke or two at the client's expense. Raising the level of their communication will help the medium avoid social situations that are not exactly comfortable.

I will say this, never a dull moment when one of these entities arrives! Many a misa has had a break in the serene at the hands of a Madama's colorful language. After that, it is better for the chairs to call for a prayer to recoup the decorum.

Native American entities, for the most part, do not mount their mediums directly. These spirits prefer to communicate through the medium by providing visions, sounds, touch, smell, and other psychic attributes. The medium will definitely feel the spirit, and may even be given a shudder or two. Conscious and aware, the spiritist will deliver the message intended by the soul.

Generally speaking, most spirits will either come through in semi-trance or physically. The above-mentioned entities are slightly different in their delivery.

CORRECT MEDIUMNISTIC ACTIONS

When the spirits get close to the medium, the chills begin in various areas of the body. Some people feel the hairs on their arms stand. Others report this in the leg area. Still others state that the hairs on their scalp and face felt like they were standing on edge. This is quite normal and proof that the spirit is overlapping the person's aura. Since we are all electrical force fields, the resultant shock can be a spinal jolt near the back of the neck. When two force fields collide, sparks fly! If new to this, the medium may experience fear. Most, though, feel an emotion akin to elation.

At this moment the medium's hands will rise and be placed slightly to the sides and back of the head, without touching. Perhaps three or four inches away is best. As the electrical sensation comes and goes, the medium's hands will then go into a synchronized, circular movement from the head, neck and outward. It is almost as if they are wrapping themselves with the spirit's aura over their own. It is a motion done very fast.

As all of this is going on, within seconds I might add, the medium will be receiving images, and word inspiration. It is then that the medium will "speak" for the entity. The spirit will greet with phrases such as, "May the peace of the Lord be here", or "Peace and Justice, Love and Charity". The entity will proceed to give the message it came to deliver and/or cleanse the aura of the person in question of any imperfections or negative vibrations. As the medium passes his/her hands over the person's aura, they will then empty them into a bowl of water. The hands will touch the lip of the bowl, not the water. The palms will feel as if they are emptying out vibrations. Once finished, the medium will then summon one of the members of his/her quadrant to clean themselves. Afterwards they will all sit, and the Mesa Blanca will continue.

This may look and sound simple, but it is far from it. Indeed, this technique may take years to master. At this point, I wish to underscore the absolute necessity for any aspiring medium to study a few mediums, and inquire about their reputations within spiritist circles. From there, and using affinity between the two, choose a mentor that will help you to grow and understand the technical skills necessary, as well as the emotional stability, in order to develop as a medium. This process is always---always---a long-term project.

The relationship between mentor and student is intense. The mentor must get deep into the student's inner being to make contact with the quadrant. The trust in the relationship is paramount to its success. And the mentor should always remember that he/she is also a student. I have learned from my students as their progress unfolds. Indeed, every entity brings a specific gift. As we elders age, we must remember that these students are the mentors of tomorrow. One day when we're in need, we will have them to turn to.

Our mediumnistic gift is not for self-edification. We must spread the seeds of this psychic gift that was granted to us by the very God we'll be facing some day. The Akashic Court will want to know what we did with our power.

TEAM WORK, NOT COMPETITION

This topic is quite dear to my heart, as well as a thorn in my side. When any mediums get together in a social setting, this theme continually dominates the conversation. You will hear words such as unity, envy, jealousy, gossip, showmanship, and humbleness.

Any misa should be run on the basis of a team of mediums against any negative or evil forces. This includes the living as well as those on the other side of the veil. There are mediums who have strayed from the calling to serve without prejudice those in need. They see their gift as a "power" to be used as a control button with their clients and spiritual godchildren. I have known of many of these charlatans who resolve only part of the client's problem, knowing full well that it's within their power to solve it quickly and permanently, even if it takes two or three sessions. This way they are constantly keeping the person dependent and constantly returning. The economics are part of this, but, even more so, is the medium's ego. They flaunt their mediumnistic abilities like an soldier showing off their weapon of choice! Ultimately, the person grows tired of a seemingly endless solution to one problem that is beginning to drain their patience as well as their purse.

The results of this can be extremely harmful to the client. Either they'll continue to manifest an unhealthy dependence on this medium, or, as is more often the case, they will leave the spiritualist world and run to a church, where the only thing church fanatics will hear will be about the negativity of mediums.

Because of this ego evil, charlatans are making us appear as the proverbial "wicked witches of the west". It's sad that our worst enemy is within our front lines. The more we root out this type of medium, the happier we will all be about our respective spiritual callings. Proper and morally sound spiritual education will discourage the development of this type of medium, which, unfortunately, has created havoc, especially in the Hispanic world.

The other very troubling cloud that sometimes lingers over our heads is gossip. Oh God Almighty! If I had a dollar for all the gossip I've heard and been caught up in over my spiritual life, I'd be a millionaire many times over! When people attend a reunion, what you hear during the misa is not to be used as social fodder. I hate to quote this terrible soul, but Hitler put it neatly: "Alone, a person can understand another, but the public, as a group, is, at best, despicable…"

Unfortunately it is all too correct. I wish that people everywhere, especially mediums, would observe the Golden Rule. No one wants their problems used as community conversation…you wouldn't like it, either. Take note all of you fellow mediums who host misas. . . Within every misa---and it's best right after the opening prayers--- forcefully remind those present that what happens in the misa, stays in the misa. Many places that have a permanent setting have even used a poster with this message. This will raise the level of comfort in those present.

By the same token, there are individuals who don't want to admit to any veracities asserted by the mediums because of the presence of others. Ladies and gentlemen, if you insist on not wanting anyone to know anything about you, then do not attend a misa, unless it's a private one just for you. We have a saying in Spanish that if you don't want the spotlight, don't walk onto the stage!

Continuing on to another very tender wound, I wish to speak about situations where witchcraft is lifted off a client in a misa. More often than not, a person knows exactly who sent the evil spirit or vibration to them. When they see and feel it lifted their emotions really come into play. Here the mediums need to use diplomacy and etiquette to the max. The person could become quite angry and swear vengeance, or they could break down in tears. Still others are left in awe that it came from whom it did.

As the proceedings move on, the chairperson should instruct the client about the workings of karma in our lives. The person must be made to refrain from returning evil for evil. When one plays with a dirty basketball, the hands are never free of the soot. If the person is to remain cleansed of the evil lifted off, they must keep their petition of justice only to the Almighty. What goes around comes around. What we living souls need to learn is that the Cosmic Clock rarely moves at the same pace as our daily time piece. God will wait until the time is ripe for the person to really feel the same pain they sent. This is not always directly at the person. People suffer most through their loved ones…and this is where spiritual justice is usually felt, even years after. But the timing must be just right so they remember why they or their loved ones are suffering now.

Lifting the evil is not the only important process. The education of keeping clean is just as critical to helping those that come in need of our Spiritual Quadrants. You will continue to see them coming back, as well as bringing others in need. Like I said before, in the Hispanic culture, nobody picks up a spiritual newspaper or magazine or website looking for people who "have a centro." Word of mouth is everything to us. It is the most trustworthy advertising in our communities.

Wrapping this area up, the most important thing for anyone hosting a misa is to promote unity, understanding, and, above all, love for one another. After all, we're all in this boat we call Earth together. Humor is a great break within the somber workings of the misa. The spirits themselves like to lighten things up every once in a while during the Great Work.

TIDBITS TO REMEMBER . . . AND FORGET!

There are incidents in misas over the past decades that never fade from memory. Some are held in awe and loving remembrance, but others are either funny or unpleasant to chew on. Drama is usually a constant visitor at all reunions, but so is laughter. Sometimes, however, very disagreeable things happen---especially when hot, Hispanic tempers flare up.

I remember a particularly tearful situation involving a young woman. She was attempting to start a new life over with her second husband. When she was called to the altar every medium in the room was receiving visions about her past. Finally, one of the mediums spoke to her quite bluntly.

"You've lost over three children, haven't you?"

After a long silence, "Yes, five times…"

"But these were not miscarriages. My spirit is telling me that these were abortions!" The medium's quadrant had her more and more agitated as the visions continued. "What's more, these abortions were paid for by your previous husband because neither one wanted children at that time, correct?"

The woman tearfully blinked as she looked around. "Yes…"

Then the spirit descended upon the medium. "May the peace of the Lord be here! Now you come! Now! You are in love again and this one wants kids, eh? All the couple of years you've been together and---nothing! Did you think these spirits would let you get away with this without paying penance? Five spirits of children, boys and girls, are standing near you and they say that not one child is coming until you do right by them!!!"

The woman started crying heavily, trying to talk. The spirit , however, was not done with her. "You must put five goblets of water, fresh, every day for nine days. You will pray the Lord's Prayer, the Hail Mary, and Glory Be… for those nine days. You will seek forgiveness from them for interrupting their lives! When fertilization takes place there are two souls entering the womb---the soul of the one coming to be born, and their guardian angel. Once this process is broken, these spirits, which have no karma, have all the power in the world to either ask to be reborn with other parents, or to stay and punish the present parents, especially the mother. Clean your heart and soul, woman! Now that you want them, they don't come! For over two years you and him have tried. Light a candle to Our Lady of Charity (La Caridad del Cobre) and hope you are forgiven! You must name each of the five children…and call them by their names forever. The first two were girls, the second two were boys, and the last was a girl."

She was speechless, as no one, not even her present husband, had known about the abortions. The spirit cleaned the woman's aura and blessed her, amid the tears, then cleaned the medium and departed. The room was heavy in silence. Her present husband was silent, yet you could feel his weight in sadness.

I instructed the woman and her new husband not to lose hope, because at no time did the spirit say things were final. Rather I implored her to do the act of penance for the nine days, to turn these spirits from foes to allies and, eventually, into guardian angels.

Later on in the year we heard from her the happy news that she was expecting. Of course she kept coming to the misas often to have her pregnancy blessed. One day this couple brought the newborn little girl to the misa for a blessing. Then it was our turn to be teary-eyed.

Halloween is in October, but I'll never forget how one July a couple of charlatans thought they'd celebrate it at one of my misas. We had just celebrated the opening prayers of a general reunion. Through the window I see this small car drive up and park. It was quite a while before I noticed a rocking movement within the parked auto. I thought my eyes were deceiving me when I saw billowing blankets of white getting out of the car.

"What the . . . ?"

Suddenly standing on my driveway were two men dressed in what they must have imagined were Arabs. Almighty Allah forgive them, I thought! What is this?

They whisked themselves into the chamber and sat towards the front of the chair arrangement.

"Why are you here in those costumes?" My sarcastic Virgo voice could not hide my creeping feelings of anger, amusement, and disdain. "Whoever sent you here did not give you correct information about what type of spiritual center I run here!"

"But our guardian spirits are Arabs. That is why we honor them with our clothing."

"Honor them?" I retorted in my loudest voice. The temple went silent. "All you're doing is materializing them. Instead of lifting them higher up on the plain of light, you are holding them down.... You don't do this to souls that are looking for progress! I don't know who helped you develop or if you're watching too many séance movies, but you certainly ain't staying here!" My shaking voice apparently drove home the point I was making.

They harrumphed their way through the door. My last vision of this tragi-comedy was of the billowing sheets through open car windows as they sped away.

Instantly the temple broke out in guffaws and laughter. Even the walls were talking incessantly... I waited until it was out of everyone's system, and I had calmed down in temperament. I then called for the

Lord's Prayer, while I sprinkled the room with holy water, especially the entrance. Let the spirits of light wash away the impure.

Then there was one of a few misas that resembled a Golden Gloves Quadrilateral! The only thing missing were the boxing gloves and the clang of the bell. God, how I have hated these types of séances and reunions that deteriorate into chapters of low-life reality shows full of screaming shenanigans.

This can happen when two mediums disagree on what is to be done with a particular person. The two or three mediums can begin arguing over what actions to take or where the problem comes from. Since it usually involves mediums who are very egotistical and "swear" they know more than anyone, it is just a short matter of minutes before we have a full-scale confrontation. Most often, the chairperson or a group of elders will step in and quite vocally shut both up. This is then followed by public reminders of the need for unity and strength, not egos that are unchained. One of the elders will probably take over the case and continue.

However, there have been times when everything fails, and diplomacy flies through the windows! At a dangerous moment like this, there have been instances of arguments, insults, threats, and people walking out in the middle of the misa! Then you have that rare, but not unknown occurrence: a physical fight that requires all to jump in and break up. The parties should be escorted out and forcefully informed to leave and not come back until they apologize to the spirits that guard the temple, not to mention the hosts!

It is up to the leadership in the temple to then calm everyone down and announce that the misa will continue. Most people will do just that, after the elders have calmed them down and even made light of the incident.

Yet, if the hour is late, or people voice discomfort with continuance, then the chairperson should end the misa, going into some sturdy closing prayers. It goes without saying that all will have to be cleaned before going home, whether with plants, incense, candles, or Florida water.

* * * * * * * *

These abbreviated examples of misas that I've attended, or hosted, I put forth as warnings… Do not attempt to run a misa until you have been trained well by an elder, and your Spiritual Quadrant has agreed that you are ready. Unfortunately, too many mediums want to fly before they can even walk! Unless you've been to many a reunion, have been trained, have co-chaired, and gotten your fingers burned a bit, do not even go there…

The rumor mill is ripe with gossip about who "fell on their face" in a misa because they had no experience and, therefore, no control. It's bad enough all the "chisme" (gossip) that pursues us from outside and inside the spiritist circles. Please don't add to it by wanting to "show out" how much you know---or don't know…!

Go at a pace that is comfortable for you during your development. This is usually measured in years, not months. There is so much to learn. First, you must use your training to learn about your field of expertise, whether it's reading, mediumship, or a mixture. Your spirits and the passing of them through you will be a huge step that will take up quite a bit of time. Then the steady attendance at misas and prayers will round out a lot of the training.

Now, we must not forget that there are spirits and saints in other religions that often involve us in one way or another. If you have come to Earth with a calling involving intense African spirits, the chances that you will have to enter either Palo Mayombe, Ocha (Santeria), the 21 Divisions (Sanse), or Voodoo are enhanced. These are other roads that complement Spiritism and contribute greatly to the growth of any medium, if they have that calling. It all depends on the makeup of the spirits in the medium's Quadrant. One cannot invent these things. Either you have a heavy African calling or not.

You may have an abundance of ecclesiastical spirits which would affect you greatly in the path you must follow, which would be quite elevated in nature. Indigenous souls keep us involved with natural healing, roots, etc.

Development is like a whole planet on its own orbit. Until you feel prepared and ready---and your spirits push you---take your time to grow fully. Remember that people will trust you with their problems. You have a responsibility to be at your best to deal with the unseen, unknown, and unspoken.

PENNIES, PESOS, AND PIGGY BANKS...

This area is one of those thorny issues that sparks all too many show-downs! The sound "ka-ching!" stirs an unseen economic hormone that usually brings out the worst in any individual or group. Within the Hispanic community there is a deeply ingrained distrust of anyone who takes advantage of their gift to accumulate wealth at the expense of those they're supposed to help.

I have heard of exorbitant amounts of money being charged for misas, readings, cleanings, and baths. Indeed, I sometimes wonder about the mental state of people who would pay such ridiculously high "donations" to any medium. Even if the client is known to be wealthy, they must be treated as a person in need first and foremost. After all, one of the unwritten commandments in the spiritist world reads: Work well on all, without prejudice of any type.

For some of the spirit works that need to be performed, there are plants, flowers, or potions necessary for the ritual to be successful. Naturally, their cost can accumulate, depending on the quantity needed. For the most part, it is the medium that will have to buy these accessories, since most of the public doesn't habitually use them and wouldn't readily know where to buy them. This can be factored at cost and passed on to the client in addition to the donation they are able to handle.

I usually charge the same as for a reading. As of 2014, the usual rate on the street for a reading is quoted as $25 to $35, more or less. Yet, we all run into people who we know cannot even afford this at the time. Well, if they wish to give a small amount, so be it. We mediums know who can or can't afford it. Just make sure that regardless of how much money well-off client makes, you charge them the same as anyone else. In our community, Latin tongues will wag plentiful. It is these tongues that are the advertising for any medium. Like I said before, Hispanics tend to shun storefront psychics, viewing them as strictly business oriented, and not very spiritual.

Many mediums charge for conducting a séance. What I've usually heard is in the range of $150 to $300, depending on how many mediums will be needed. However, there are just as many mediums who will not charge for misas. Misas are viewed as part of the calling by most spiritists. If you really are a follower of the modern spiritist movement as instructed by Allan Kardec, the father of today's spiritism, you will view the reunions as a task of a missionary. I feel there should be no charge, or a nominal amount. If so, it is for the actual working spiritists, who pass their quadrant and perform the work and cleaning.

Now, to curl your hair! I have heard of outrageous amounts being demanded for the celebration of a misa. I heard through the grapevine that someone was charged $1,000 for the act, and, if anyone lifted a dark entity, that would be an extra $1,000! Good golly…! No one ever read about the merchants in the temple? Even Jesus took to the whip on this!

No, indeed…. It pains me to hear this, especially in light of our economic tribulations. People forget karma. You can't perpetrate this and not expect it to come back to you and bite you on the wrong side of your anatomy! We are dealing with a sacred trust, people! Our clients come to us with intimate problems that takes courage to entrust to another. Our actions will greatly impact their lives. Families, friendships, even marriages, will hang by a thread, waiting for the word from our spirit messengers upon which they will act on faith.

Many of these charlatans have caused vast numbers of people to abandon the spiritualist camp and seek safety in churches, mosques, or synagogues. Little do they know, however, that tithing or other expected donations await them. In short, we must remember that the medium's very existence is to be that bridge between the material and spiritual sides of the veil of life.

Many will wonder, then, at the cost of entering one of the African faiths, such as Ocha (Santeria), Palo Mayombe, Voodoo, Sanse, Obiya, etc. These are ceremonies that involve great costs. It is sometimes a seven-day ritual. During this time, provisions have to be made for the cooks, the many participants, the clothing, and the rent of the place to be used. This can be costly because of all the things that must be bought to do it right.

For any continued talk on finances, I would appreciate you direrct the questions at the members of these different religions. Spiritism is the first of the steps in any medium's life. That is why I have dedicated my life to assist in the development of good mediums. God knows, there are never enough of them…

RECIPES FROM THE QUADRANT'S PANTRY

Our temples or consultation rooms often resemble a pharmacy. In most Botanicas, the spiritual supply stores, you will be able to purchase every conceivable object necessary for all types of spirit work. What you will read here is a small fraction of all the available workings. As we speak, there are new recipes being prescribed.

Breaking Chains . . .

Part of lifting off the negativity of either a dark entity or curses from another person can often involve the ordering of a "breaking", better known in Spanish or Portuguese as a "rompimiento". There are a myriad of ways this can be performed by a medium. Basically, there is a general formula that is followed.

1. There should be a location chosen that is appropriate for this act. It can be the woods, the river bank, the ocean beach, or inside a temple.
2. The client should wear old clothing that has been worn at least once, so that their essences are still within the cloth. This includes underwear, pants, t-shirt, and socks. Footwear is not included in this rite. The client should be advised that none of their old clothing will be spared.

3. They should bring with them in a bag, clean or new white clothing. Whatever they're going to be dressed in at the end of the "breaking" must be white, including the towel.
4. Once the person arrives, the medium will have the following tools ready: scissors, candle, incense, a huge bowl or pail with holy water and herbs, and... privacy.
5. It is wise to have another medium there, or to have the client bring an observer of their own. Due to the rather intimate nature of a "breaking", everyone must be of the same gender. If this is an impossibility, then a huge, white blanket can be used as a veil while the presiding medium instructs the other mediums, who are the same gender as the client, where to cut and rip the clothing, bathe and dress them.
6. Just before the actual ceremony, opening prayers should be given for all the quadrants involved, especially that of the client. Once the incantations are over with, while praying and imploring the spirits' guidance, the presiding medium will begin to cut and forcibly rip off each layer of clothing until the person is in their birthday suit.
7. Now, with great care and responsibility, the medium begins to pour small amounts of the potion onto the head of the client. It is best to use a natural receptacle such as half a coconut shell or gourd for this. The medium will continue to pour the water over the body until they get to the feet. There should be a portable tub the person can stand in to collect the falling water if you're indoors.
8. Now the client will be allowed to dry themselves off and dress up in their white clothing. The water, meantime, will be discarded into the Earth, which holds all there is and cleans all there is.
9. The ceremony will end with the closing prayers. The client or another participant will take the old clothing parts in

a bag, with a few coins, and dispose of them far from the medium's house in a public garbage disposal.

Some words of advice on the "breakings" to really ponder before you perform them. Some people are way too squeamish to get down to their birthday suit. For these people, you may make the exception and allow them to wear a bathing suit, which they must wash thoroughly upon getting home. It is wise to have a third or even fourth or fifth party present. This leaves you in the clear as far as any rumblings later on.

Of course there are some of our godchildren who have so much confidence and trust that it can be done one-on-one. Indeed, some would prefer it.

The spirituality of the "breaking" must be of the highest level of devotion. The medium must see the need of the supplicant, not the body. It is always best that all the details be discussed. Rule of thumb: everyone should be of the same gender, if possible. This is why it is in your interest, as a medium, to foment a circle of godchildren that are both male and female. Trust me, there is plenty of work to go around.

El Santiguo…

This term, "el santiguo", is applied to a physical blessing of the person with holy oil or water. More often than not it is used on babies, children, and ill adults. Not every medium has this gift. It depends solely on the nature of the spirits in your quadrant.

It must be established through other mediums and spirits that you are protected by a spirit that gives you this gift. It involves the calming of small babies who sometimes see and might be bothered by spirits, or entities that aren't exactly made of light and sunshine! The "santiguo"---sanctification---of this infant will come after the medium has been contacted by the parents. He or she will proceed to the crib where the infant sleeps. There the medium will begin with prayers and begin using holy water or minute amounts of anointing oil and draw seven crosses with the index finger from the crown of the head to the soles of the feet. The palms of the hands will be included. If the baby permits and isn't extremely fussy, this should be repeated on the back of his body as well.

The crib should then be lightly sprinkled with the holy water or oil. Vibrational passes over the crib should be performed through the medium's palms. This can take a few minutes, or until the medium "receives" that the crib has been radiated sufficiently with blessed vibrations. The medium should be visualizing the room free of any soul that is not a guardian angel of the baby in question. Sooner, rather than later, the child will drift off and get a good night's sleep, along with the weary parents…

One thing to always check on is that, if you're using oil, make sure the baby is not allergic. I like to use only holy water on infants because of this. I reserve the oil for older children and adults who would know by then if they were allergic to any ingredient in the anointing oil. It pays to be thorough.

My Innards Need a Flush!

We've all heard how dangerous ingesting cursed concoctions can be. They are some of the hardest spells to be rid of. The depth of the curse in a drink or food will dictate the way it will be removed. It is important to note that the majority of these ingested toxins are not accompanied by a spiritual presence. Usually, they are prepared and then the person "prays" an incantation over it and concentrates on the intended recipient. This is akin to an astral projection so that as the targeted person eats or drinks the prepared offering, the vibrations over it will begin to do their intended work within the digestive system.

As the food or drink are broken down by the stomach and neighboring organs, the curse begins to take hold, causing havoc on the person's health and daily life. Often the victim will visit a doctor, only to find that the symptoms come and go. The medical personnel will usually not be able to rid the victim of the spell. In time, someone within the Hispanic community will suggest that they seek the help of a "brujero" or "bruja" to remove the spell that obviously doesn't respond to medical treatment.

Now begins the diagnosis as to what action merits incorporation in the lifting of this malevolence. It should begin with a visit for a reading. Somewhere during the reading, the medium will pick up on the physical ingestion. The client can openly tell the medium what they suspect to be their problem from the start of the reading. The medium will then confirm the presence or not. If not, they'd better find another physician. But, if things have reached this point, it's a sure bet there is a curse within them.

Depending on the type of spirits involved with the medium, a decision is reached on how to rid the victim of the curse. I have often had to employ direct spirit possession to remove the vibrations of the curse. This entails having your quadrant "mount" you and your hands will travel over the affected areas picking up these dark vibes. They will be "deposited" into a clear glass bowl of water. The medium's hands will not actually touch the water. Rather they will empty the negative rays by carefully banging onto the lip of the bowl, as if you were shaking loose an object from your hands into the water. It will be repeatedly done until the spirit has finished cleaning the person. The spirit will finish by giving a blessing to the aura of the person and announcing their blessing upon them.

If it is determined that the curse is rather bland and not really that effective, the spirit of the medium might, instead, prescribe certain types of teas. Rue, mint, basil, rosemary, anisette, to name a few, are staples in cleaning the body of spiritual toxins. Blessed black espresso is also a possible instrument to cleanse a body that's been attacked.

This brings me to what my mother would always caution me about. "Always look directly into the coffee cup when given black coffee. If you see your face like a mirror, drink it, if not, make believe you're allergic, but don't drink it by any means!"

Words of wisdom. Black coffee can be a flush or a weapon.

In one of the African religions, specifically Palo Mayombe, there is a prepared liquor, laced with specific additives, that will definitely burn out all witchcraft attempted through ingestion. Trust me, that's one flush you won't forget!

Sweeping the Air

One of the most common of all prescriptions is the cleaning of the home or business. In the Hispanic community a house or a place of business, even a website, is treated as an individual, living agent, complete with its own vibrations.

When I walk into any home, the first thing I begin picking up are the vibes of the home. Is it light and positive? Peaceful? Or does the heaviness of darkness hit me like a thrown sack of bricks? Are there any specific areas more negative than others?

In any home the central spiritual axis is rooted in the kitchen, with secondary ones in the bathrooms. These are the main sources of power as well as the first targets in any living quarters. It matters not whether it's an apartment, single-family house, or studio. These areas of concentration are the same.

When asked to clean a home, most of my tools are usually three coconuts from the grocery---the hairy, little brown ones, not with their outside greenish casing. To these are added flowers, usually white chrysanthemums, carnations, daisies or even roses. A bottle of holy water, another of Florida water, white household candles, and a bunch of herbs. If there is no one asthmatic or allergic in the house, incense and a cigar can be used. The herbs are usually the bitter type. Vencedor, Rompe Zaraguey, Quita Maldicion are but a few that can be used. Translated, respectively, they are Conqueror, Breaking a Jinx, Curse Removal. With names like that I'm sure you'll wish to have quite a thick bunch. Most botanicas will have them or you can order through them. However, if you know a good herbalist in the community or, even better, an Osainista, things will work best with very fresh, newly cut herbs. An Osainista is a person in Santeria who is consecrated as an herbalist to the saint, Osain, pronounced [oh-SINE]. They are few and far between, and they are treasured in the Hispanic community, Spritist, Santero, Palero alike. These elderly gentlemen have devoted their lives to the study of plants and their spiritual and material properties. You rarely see any but an older man, since it takes so long to, first, be consecrated to Osain, and then to spend a lifetime studying until you are ready to be accepted as a full-blown Osainista.

When the cleaning is to begin, the owners of the home should be there. To clean a home, one medium can do it, if need be. However, I usually like to take two more with me, at least. Six eyes see more than two.

The prayers are invoked for the cleaning. These prayers are directed at the quadrants of the mediums, the owners of the home, and all entities that might be dwelling there, from before the family moved in. Then, the mediums will line up by the front door. I will lead with the coconut to be pushed throughout the house by using only my feet. The others will follow, some holding the candles, another the herbs, incense, some one puffing the billowing out the cigar smoke. The family will follow.

All the while that the procession is winding through the house, the Lord's Prayer, Hail Mary, and Glory Be to God will be repeated. The coconut is for picking up like a vacuum cleaner. As it is gently nudged by my bare feet, it will direct me to specific areas and corners in each room. I may wind up asking the homeowner about an incident I pick up that occurred there. Other times I might be given information, such as faulty electrical wiring or plumbing problems that could manifest themselves. Often there will be warnings concerning preventing of fire.

Major concentration must be placed when cleansing the kitchen and bathrooms. All walk-in closets, outdoor porches, patios, and the garage are also to be cleaned.

When we all have arrived back to the front door, a plastic bag will be on the floor in front of the door. The coconut will be kicked into it, lifted, at least three coins will be placed inside, then it will be knotted up and put outside the door to be disposed of later.

There will be a small discussion between the mediums and the family of what was "found" and what, if anything, needs to be done at this time. If any of the mediums have picked up on a negative entity, it should be "lifted" there by a medium capable of performing this act. If not, then the closing prayers are done and we end it.

The family might offer a donation and to partake in snacks and soft drinks. Liquor or beer are never to be served in any spiritual activity!

Upon leaving, someone will volunteer to take the bag with the infested coconut and dispose of into a wooded area, or a public garbage can. If the spirits indicate a rather far destination, a donation for the person's gas should be made, though usually it's quite close.

The Romantic Puppeteer ... Run the Other Way!

You will always run into what I call the "den of love junkies". The hassles of the heart are a never-ending problem since time immemorial. Many a headache have I received at the hands of a frustrated lover! I'm not going to bore you with an example of thousands of forms to hold or push away a love interest. Humanity must still learn deep spiritual lessons concerning love and its place among karma, destiny, and reincarnation.

Many times those people we fall in love with we have known romantically in another life. The love between souls often goes so deep that many incarnations take place between them. They can meet as a couple, parent and child, siblings, a couple again, but as the opposite genders they've been, and so forth.

This explains that feeling of love at first sight. Knowledge of people we meet for the first time can often unnerve us. Soul mates who meet "accidentally" can experience a myriad of emotions, many of them troubling. However, see these feelings through. It can be the beginning of a great friendship or romance, regardless of the genders involved.

Often the negative aspect of soul mates will appear. A former mate who has not incarnated will latch on to the aura of the targeted loved one. If this spirit refuses to let go or positively accompany their former partner, they can cause major interference in the person's life. In many instances I have had clients who were faced with a spirit of a past mate that was causing upheavals in their present relationship, including family ties. Sometimes this entity will respond well to prayer and candles in their name. this will help them to see their new existence without their former mate. They might choose to stay and be part of the guardian angels of the quadrant. Often these spirits will announce to a widow or widower that they bless their new union with another, a situation that helps all involved.

However, if the jealousy and anger of the spirit are causing suffering in the client, then that former mate must be treated the same as a dark entity and, in the process of the misa, will be removed and sent upward towards the "spiritual schools" where entities of light will help them understand and accept their new destiny, as ordained from Above.

All in all, the medium must be astute when dealing with a client who wants to mend a marriage or other romantic union. Everyone paints themselves as the martyr in this. What the medium's quadrant must do, is really dig in to see where the real source of the problem lies. It can be interference from the other side, a mate who likes to "roam", or the client's jealousy. Regardless of the cause, the medium's task is to help the client see both the cause and the solution, which might not always be what they wish for.

Avoid, at any cost, being drawn in to tying a person to another. Everyone has at least one guardian angel who will sooner or later send back what was sent. Result: a worse situation than before. People must learn that love cannot be forced. If there is a change in a relationship, both parties must remember that each is a world unto themselves. Love is a full-time job. But it is also a material situation that strictly calls for the parties involved to act on the material plane and not cause a shift in the cosmic patchwork. Again, when you see that a client is obsessed in love matters beyond what you have been able to read and do, start edging away from that person before you're drawn into a spiritual war that will come back to haunt you and your quadrant!

TOMORROW'S NEWS TONIGHT

Events that make headlines have often been predicted at a Mesa Blanca by spirits who have a deep interest in the safety of the state of humanity. To be sure, when catastrophic events are going to occur anywhere on Earth, there is a phenomenon observed that involves hundreds of people being entrusted this information. During the summer of 2001, there were many reports of people who dreamt of the Twin Towers bombing. It was given in slightly altered ways. There were those who saw wars, others an inferno, or people falling.

At my home in January of that year, we were celebrating a misa with my family and spiritual godchildren present. During one of my quadrant's arrival, my guardian angel, no less, came through. He lamented that the 21st Century would be a century of darkness, not the plain of light on the horizon that so many had dreamed of. Further, he said, that summer a war would begin when a large city would be attacked from the air and buildings would fall, touching off a long, painful war. This entity happens to be of Arabic origins!

Summer lasts until September 22nd. The morning of the eleventh, right after those heart-wrenching attacks, I received a phone call from my oldest daughter who nervously reminded me of what my spirit had announced nine months ago! I was further shocked. I had completely forgotten that January night. Those that know me well, are aware that I always ask God to hide into my deep memory all that goes on in any misa. This helps to avoid any slip of a tongue that could cause future misunderstandings.

I was shaken to the core as my Arab spirit's words flooded back into my head. This entity comes from a very ancient time. Being the guardian angel of my quadrant, his main responsibility is to open the gates for the other working spirits. It is not often that the head of the quadrant comes through to speak or work. It must have been very difficult for him to communicate these events, since they involved many of from his cultural roots.

I prayed heavily that day, and just as was said, this century has been anything but light. Darkness seems to be enveloping the world with increasing violence. Even the climate is evolving into a threat to our very existence.

But there are other events that have equally been foreseen in spiritist reunions. Politicians secretly like to visit a trusted medium for help either in their election campaigns or guidance while performing their duties to their electorate. For any medium, this can be risky if you don't stick to your guns and tell it like it is. All people, not just politicos, feel they are in the right all the time. It is up to the spirits to keep them anchored in reality.

Weather events occupy a high level on the list of worldly problems helped by spiritist mediums. On or about the start of hurricane season, which begins on June 1st and lasts through November 30th, I am kept busy answering the eternal question, "Is one coming?" In my case, I usually receive this news in a dream. Sometimes I am visited in my sleep with this information early in the year, other times during the spring. All I'll say is, we should all pray for average rainfall. This keeps the oceans a bit cooler, a fact that keeps storms down. Droughts are traditionally broken by storms. The global warming that is wreaking havoc with our climate, promises to bring us more powerful cyclonic activity. Again, where there is good rainfall, the chances are dim for these monsters to visit.

Once in a blue moon you'll have a medium make headlines for predicting a major global event. Me, I feel the really major events are the ones in our private lives that help us grow. No medium starting their development should have delusions of grandeur. A true medium does not get rich or famous when assisting our fellow man or woman. This is the greater calling, the real brick-by-brick building of a better world.

THE DANGERS OF TRANSLATIONS

This subject rapidly brings my blood to a boil! Many of the prayers and books that are originally in Spanish, French, or Portuguese, have been translated word for word, literally… That is *not* translation in any way, shape, or form. Different languages are part of a larger culture. Within a culture there is a particular way of thinking and viewing life that, when translated word for word, loses all sense of reality. One must translate the *idea* of what is being said or written. It may not be exact in words, but the thoughts will convey the action the writer or speaker wishes to convey in a manner that promotes understanding and appreciation.

One of my favorite pieces of exemplary mis-translation is a key prayer that is essential in any Mesa Blanca. In Spanish it is titled, "Plegaria del Naufrago." A good English translation would be "Castaway's Plea on the Sea of Life" or "Adrift Upon the Waves of Spirit". This prayer-poem, which comes directly from the devotional prayer book of Allan Kardec, are the words of a person who calls upon God to save him from the sea of life. A sea where every wave represents temptations. They are begging for salvation from drowning in the evils and torment of this world.

That said, I once picked up an English version of the book in a botanica and was horrified to see this prayer titled, "The Shipwreck"! What darn shipwreck? The entire poem is about a person struggling with life's trials and tribulations and the eternal struggle between right and wrong. This alleged translation reads like a three-year-old wrote it. As I read through the words I cringed. Nothing made sense. No wonder Anglos are left empty and puzzled after reading this type of caca-juice! Who wouldn't be? People are looking for inspiration and this idiot-school translation talks about a shipwreck?!!! The business powers that be should be hounding the publishers for a real translation. One that leaves the Anglo with the same thought as the Hispanic.

Allan Kardec, the father of modern-day spiritism, must be watching this from the other side in dismay. One day, someone will take on the huge task of translating the entire devotional prayer book. There are many more complex prayers and long, intense poems that will require many heads indeed to correctly translate the message. Work that should be well paid for, considering the depth of the project.

Allan Kardec was the pen name of Hippolyte Leon Denizard Rivail. He was born in Lyon, France, on October 3, 1804, and passed on in Paris, France, on March 31, 1869, of an aneurysm. He was a teacher and educator who is known as the systematizer of Spiritism. In addition, Mr. Kardec laid this foundation with the five books of the Spiritist Codification. Subjects taught by him: mathematics, physics, chemistry, astronomy, physiology, comparative anatomy, and French. In 1831 he was inducted into the Royal Academy of Arras. He organized and taught free courses for the underprivileged. In 1832 he was married to Amelie Gabrielle Boudet.

Allan Kardec's grave is at the Paris cemetery, Cimetiere du Pere Lachaise. It is a heavily visited site. The inscription reads: "To be born, die, again be reborn, and so progress unceasingly, such is the law." Words for every soul to live by.

Every medium should read about Allan Kardec. His many books about spiritism are eye-openers for those researching the roots and foundation for their development. Eternally will his flame light the way for us. Embattled humanity keeps clawing at the soil of life, looking for truth and a way to help save the planet. May the Enlightened break through from their higher planes, to instill within us the knowledge that will take us on a new course. A course where many of the doubts as to why things happen will be dispelled. Harmony will be the tool used to promote understanding during those times of trial. Understanding karma and reincarnation will bring about true justice and love, one life at a time…

THOUGHTS AND PRAYERS

Magic Kingdom

I often drift onto an astral plane while awake and engaged in other activities. Once in a blue moon I regress to my very early childhood. We lived in the Bronx, in New York City, in the southern portion of the borough that so many Puerto Ricans flocked to from the overflowing Barrio (Spanish Harlem) in Manhattan. I would take advantage of my outdoor playtime on Fox Street, and wander off a few blocks down to the local botanica. My mother, of course, was kept in the dark about these visits. She would have polished my "haini" had she known! My mom had always been afraid of the spiritist world. Yet, when she was pregnant with me in her womb, my great-aunt, a blind midwife and healer, had told her she would give birth to a medium. My mother almost fainted with fear.

At the entrance to the botanica, which had three steps to climb at the front door, there was always a chair occupied by the owner when the store was empty. Every time I passed the botanica, he would give me a smile and a knowing look. He "knew" me, I thought then. It never frightened me, as I never felt any malice in his stare.

But that lazy, summer afternoon he suddenly addressed me, "You can come inside and see whatever you want. Just don't touch anything…"

My nose was picking up the sweet perfume of herbs, oils, extracts, and incense. My instincts moved me forward, and I entered a magical world where I felt like a traveler returning home from a long journey. I never delete from memory the sight of the fresh, green herbs in water. They instantly caught my eye. I slowly breathed in their subtle scent.

I then toured every aisle and nook in the botanica, marveling at the seven-day candles in their glass casings. Many of them were multicolored and others had images on labels of the saints and Jesus and other symbols. Then there were the bottles and bottles of oils, perfumes, and potions. There were seemingly endless rows of these small bottles on the shelves. Adjoining them were all kinds of soaps used in spiritual baths.

"I've been here before," I thought. "This place and other like it is not new to me."

Suddenly, I could hear my mother's voice in my head, and I waved goodbye to the owner and sped off to our tenement. Without looking up, I ran right into my neighbor, my mother's cousin, of all people! I knew she was a medium who often had plenty of people in her apartment, next to ours! My secret's out!

However, she only smiled, patted my head, and told me not to worry. It would be our secret. As I looked back, I saw her climbing the three steps to the botanica, greeting the owner who stared at me again.

All that evening I was afraid my mother would see my secret on my face. She didn't. My co-conspirators made my future visits possible, playing lookout. . . . Childhood…

Equality

There is no place for prejudice in spiritism, except as a karmic lesson. Anyone can be chosen by the Almighty to be blessed with this gift. No race, gender, or economic level has any special place in mediumship at all.

Indeed, this even applies to religious affiliations. Spiritism is not a religion, rather a philosophy of life. A medium can be Catholic, Protestant, Jewish, Hindu, Muslim, Buddhist, or any myriad of religions on the planet. The irony is that most, if not all, discriminate against mediums. It boils down to their systems of control, the common denominator for all organized religions. Yet, the silver cord of spirit is the only universal link among humanity. The so-called "occult" is found in differing ways in every society known to us. One day reality will enter religious leaders' minds and they will realize that their respective religions will be enhanced by the inclusion and acceptance of all mediums. It will do quite a lot to eliminate the charlatans that currently give us such a bad reputation.

Why Me?

The constant question heard from developing mediums. I have to help them understand this concept where those that are not inclined toward the spiritual path are pushed and cajoled by everyday occurrences to walk it. God usually gives this gift to those who don't want it or are afraid of it. In His plan is assuredly the desire to keep us humble as we grow in knowledge. Those that are always looking for the gift that they view as a power tool, are usually overlooked. The few that make it either become a poor example for other mediums, or the legendary conduits of evil.

It is all-important to remember that we mediums are servants of humanity. We are charged with the mission of contributing to the welfare of our loved ones, as well as those we are not familiar with. Be they poor, rich, male, female, culturally different, or from any station in life, they must be given the same service on an equal footing. To do otherwise is to condemn yourself to karma that will cause a serious setback to your soul, and cause you to repeat incarnations that would otherwise be unnecessary.

Cane-Cutting Cleansing

Some of the most beloved spirits are those that were slaves, and worked on sugar plantations. These male entities share some common traits. They were, of course, strong of body and mind. Machetes were the tool of necessity. They all share a love of black coffee, sweet, and white rum or firewater, as well as cigars. These three items provided the necessary mental and emotional break from their tedious, day-long work. As a result these items are staples to have when a person comes for a cleansing or breaking off of negative vibrations.

When any of these entities are being used, the medium will have laid out a bottle of white rum or firewater. If it's firewater (agua ardiente), make sure it does not come with anisette. Some do, and the souls of these African spirits don't like it. In addition there should be at least a couple of cigars, the original, smelly type, if you know what I mean! (Smile) You may round this list out with white candles, cleansing kerchiefs, and a machete.

One thing about the use of machetes. If you aren't comfortable or adept at using them, replace this with replicas, such as wooden machetes, if possible. Plan C would be to eliminate the machete altogether and have the spirit rely on the vibrationary force in lieu of the great harvester.

As the cleansing begins with prayers, the spiritist uses the household candle to trace the person's aura. It should be held some three inches from their body. Keep a watchful eye not to bring the flame too close to the clothing or hair. Next, sprinkle any of your potions that you are accustomed to on the blade of the machete, invoking the power of God and the spirit or saint you are working with. Put the blade on the client's head and start to work your way down the side, outlining their body, which should be standing with their arms and legs open like an "X", palms facing up. Once you reach the floor, slam the machete down so it can release what has been "scraped" off the aura. Start again from the top on the other side. Repeat over the front and then the back of the body. Finally, because the genital area is one that collects many vibes, from the floor up to and briefly, touching the genital area with the machete, bring it slamming down.

Once done, present the machete to the client, in a ritualistic manner, holding the machete with two hands, and have them kiss the blade in thanks. Next, you kiss the blade, thank your spirit guardian, and return the machete to its proper resting place.

Now use the blessing kerchief to clean the person, and once done, offer a prayer of thanks. Exchange views as to what the person and you "saw" during the cleansing. It will be quite an eye opening clue as to where the negativity came from or was picked up at.

Upon the Seas

Oh mio, Yemaya, mother of all and goddess of the oceans,
Grant me safe passage, be it to the land of tears.
Over your waters, pristine and clear, remember my face in your heart so dear.

I feel the drumming from the dark deep, chanting lament for Africa's embrace.
Songs of prayer crash upon sands. Whispers in the palms from gentle breeze.
Children playing, mothers cooking, fathers counseling---music to my ears.

I feel the kicks and life within, my heart heavy with foreboding pain.
Warned of what would be, how can we stay free?
The clang of chains dragging down my future dreams so dear.

This soul within me yearns for daylight. Alas, sunshine shrouded in gray.
Hark! Are those children singing? Choirs of creatures and angels deep,
Calls from whales, seals, and porpoises near!

The children's chants grow louder still, eardrums pumping, I lean to listen.
Mirror of water, faces so clear. And then, a shadow, a face so dear.
The woman's features melt over mine, the Mother's eyes, ever so clear.

"Come," they beckon, "my child and yours. Save him from a fate of whips!"
My heart pounds beats to the dance of freedom. I lean out arms and tilt.
Into the liquid world I dive, feeling the embrace of love sincere. . .

The sigh of the sea speaks over the shouts. "Another!" with fierce croak.
Eyes with longing look back toward the east, searching, yearning, moaning.
The chants rise to the heavens, "Oh mio, Yemaya… mother so dear…"

And so, the Middle Passage is cluttered and foaming with souls
Who sought freedom within the waters, rather than face a land of chains.
The griot * watched the scene unfold; a new story memorized clear.

The route was plowed by thousands of ships, heavy with sobs and iron.
All the while Yemaya counted and embraced the souls who swam by,
Back to the heaven in their homeland---Africa---a refuge from fear.

Centuries have passed, storms have raised the ocean deep,
Disturbing the bones of those voices that whisper their stories,
Of courage over fear, justice over evil, the angels carry pride on their spears.

The creaking of the wood on the boats haunts us still.
From the depths and from the heights, the choir chants a song of love.
"Africa…" the cry is clear. "Let us never bow to fear!"

—Florencio Guevara's Spirit Quadrant

*griot – [gree – OH] An African storyteller who was a walking encyclopedia of information about the tribal culture, holidays, and legends. There are very few still alive today.

Some Important Prayers Used At A Mesa Blanca (My Personal Translations)

At the Opening of the Misa

We pray to Our Lord to send us spirits of light to assist us, to keep away those that would induce us erroneously, and provide the necessary light to recognize the difference between truth and falsehoods. Remove from us all malevolent souls, material or spiritual, who would cause discord among us and deviate the group from our love and kindness towards all.

Good spirits who grace us with your presence; educate and make us receptive to your advice. Steer us away from egotism, pride, envy, and jealousy. Inspire us with indulgence, benevolence toward others, present or absent, friends and enemies. Through charity, humility, and abnegation let us always acknowledge your healthy influences.

For the mediums who are responsible to transmit your lessons, give them awareness of the sanctity and gravity of the task they have before them. If there are persons here who have come with negative intentions, oh good spirits, open their eyes and may God forgive their intentions. We pray, especially, that our spirit guides assist and watch over us. Amen.

Prayer for Peace in the Home (A must/traditional)

Dear Lord, I am mortal, like any other, and perhaps more sinful than most. But, having faith in Your mercy and desiring to walk the path of righteousness, repentant, I seek redemption. I understand, Lord, that through your all-powerful Presence, we are never abandoned and Your helping hand is forever extended toward us. I lift my thoughts to You and ask for the bread of Peace in my home; for troubled souls, peace; for the submission of tyrants, Peace. Through the sublime Holy Spirit let us drink from the fountain of Peace. Oh Blessed Sacrament, You, who taught us Peace through your pilgrimage in this world, conserve my family in harmony and give me Peace during my tribulations. May Peace flow throughout the sanctuary that is my home. Amen.

For the Mediums

Almighty God, permit the spirits of light to assist me in all of the communications I seek. May positive light illuminate my guardian angels and induce them toward correct actions. If I should stray from the path of light, take my gift away before I do anything that will bring about my karmic punishment.

Let me not fall into becoming a tool of evil spirits. May I be overcome with a sense of charity toward my fellow mediums. Should I fall into an erroneous path, permit them to counsel me, and cause me to see their words as balm and course correction for my mediumship.

For the Guardian Angels and Protective Spirits

Oh prudent and benevolent spirits, messengers from God, whose mission is to assist humanity and lead us through the path of goodness. Sustain us on our journey through life's tests, and let me not complain as I travel it. Detain any of our negative thoughts and deny entities of the dark access to our souls. Illuminate me, that I may know my own defects, separate from my eyes the veil of pride that would not permit me to see those defects and correct them. And to you, my guardian angel, _____, and all of my other protective spirits who have a vested interest in my well-being, I implore your benevolence. May God grant us all grace through His teachings, delivered by all of you. Amen.

And this, dear reader, is what I think should be the translation of "Plegaria del Naufrago" (A Castaway's Plea)!

A Castaway's Plea

Turn your eyes, my Lord,
Upon this unhappy being
Let me not be buried
Within the waves of the sea.

Give me strength and courage
To be saved from the abyss,
Give me grace, as always,
With the greatness of Your mercy.

If I, but a frail sailboat,
Because of my vanity and pride,
The human ocean have navigated,
Following only its pleasures of flesh.

MESA BLANCA

Allow me, Lord, to return
And stand firm on Your continent,
Fervently taking oath
As a Christian of faith.

If, through my heavy-handedness,
I floundered over the foam,
Daring Your tempest,
As waves of truth rise up.

I promise from this day forward
Not to have the audacity
To choose not to listen
To those that suffer within evil.

And continuing my way
I have had no shame
To ridicule the lighthouse
Showing me Your safe harbor.

I swear to you, my Lord,
Never to laugh at that light
That shines over the cross,
In Your beloved Son's grace.

You, oh God of my soul,
Who listens to the suffering,
You see my repentance
For what my life was like.

Save me, dear God, save me
And give me, before I answer for my actions,
The precise time,
For my repentance. Amen.

Conclusion of the Mesa Blanca

We thank the good spirits who have communicated with us. May we be able to put into practice those teachings they have imparted to us, and that as we leave for our homes, may we feel fortified with the Golden Rule, and the love of those near and dear to us.

May these teachings, likewise, have served to enlighten the spirits who suffer in ignorance and evil that visited this reunion. Over them we implore the mercy of God. Amen.

Thoughts Have Wings

My life as a medium has been anything but easy. I constantly am engaged in conversations with potential mediums who are always curious about the time it may take them to develop. If I had a dollar for every one of these dialogues I'd be quite well off!

The only answer that I could conceivably offer is that it takes whatever amount of time your quadrant receives from you. All spirits need one basic thing: prayer. Without it, or with but token syllables, do not expect to educate your spirits and have them grow. This is a gift---and a cross!

Because birds of a feather tend to flock together, mediums are sometimes lulled into believing that all global inhabitants possess the gift of mediumship. Nothing could be further from the truth. We are far and few within any society. Part of the trials I went through was acceptance from my family. My parents were sometimes at wit's end and contemplated "what to do with me." Having a child who would predict to others, interpret dreams, and see the non-living was not exactly relished within the family circle.

I know what you're thinking. True, in Hispanic society, particularly Puerto Rican families, spiritism was widely known, practiced and used. Rare is the person who does not consult a spiritist at some time in their life.

Of course, in social circles it is rarely spoken of unless those present are within the spiritist world. It is often the subject of much scolding by spirits in the misas. They don't take kindly to people who always put down spiritism as backward and superstitious rantings of "low class poor people." Entities know the gravity of blocks on the path of a quadrant of souls that have a mission to accomplish.

Both the spirit of the person within the material body and their spirit quadrant have been before the Akashic Court. The many lives of the aforementioned are reviewed and judged there. It is determined what type of destiny must be tackled in the next incarnation, both as living and spirit students of life. Depending on the necessity of those involved, the Akashic Records will determine the matching of incarnate to entity, providing a common ground for all parties to have the opportunity in the coming life that they couldn't in others to conquer tests put before them. This enables all to achieve progress and movement through the vigorous participation in the Cycle of Birth, Death, and Rebirth. I view this like a never ending upside down pyramid that grows larger and larger as you progress upwards toward our ultimate goal: union with God. Becoming, finally, after thousands of lives, a spark of the Almighty's Light is the foremost priority we should possess.

By living the Golden Rule, and adhering to basic rules of positive living, we can be constantly improving our status within incarnations, and preparing ourselves for helping our fellow humans achieve the same progress we want for ourselves.

Another inquiry I deal with is the age-old question of, "Why does God permit these things to happen?" Once again, the word *test* comes to mind. It is vital that children not be led to believe that God won't allow negative things to occur. Focus on the need to live facing up to the tests of life in enabling children to face the facts surrounding trials and tribulations in life as they grow.

Launching Pads

The making of a good medium may involve many different scenarios of growth. Many mediums-to-be are attracted toward Tarot cards or the Spanish Brisca cards. Crystal balls are another major draw, though cost of a legitimate crystal ball makes using water for scrying the most popular starting point of all. Still others are attracted to the Runes. Then, there's the Chinese I Ching to open up the spiritual antenna. Regardless of which path chosen, each represents a gateway to mediumship which I value very much.

No one is born channeling spirits. The ability is dormant, awaiting the correct time and scenario. The more the potential medium reads and develops psychic skills with the aforementioned tools, the better and sooner they'll be ready for further growth into mediumship. Which tools to choose? Your quadrant will have that answer. Whatever culture they knew in their last incarnation will directly affect your attraction to a particular psychic tool. Your spirits may, in addition to being in the culture, have been participants in the use of them.

Many an entity takes credit, when channeled, for the medium's knowledge and usage of, for example, the Tarot. Most probably, the medium will work with the deck of Tarot cards like the spirit who they channel. This will bring an added boost to the accuracy of that medium's readings.

However, there is a warning to this: don't overstretch your reach or, like an octopus with outstretched legs, you'll fall flat on your ego!

Development must be orderly, a skill at a time. Too many young mediums want to fly before they even know how to crawl... Once you've chosen the first psychic tool to study and be skilled at, stick to it. Don't try to do three and four things at a time because they seem easy at first. Failure is a road paved with ego and frustration. Its origin is quite simple. You must not be the one who pushes pell mell into these studies in order to impress with how much you know and all the different ways you possess to deliver answers.

What comes to mind always is the race between the rabbit and the tortoise. Speed caused the rabbit to see and learn nothing, and still not achieve his goal. The tortoise took one step at a time. Slowly and with deliberate step, the tortoise mended his way, It enabled him to assimilate all the lessons involved and practice well, honing the diamond, if you will. This greatly influences the depth of your preparation.

Reading. If I've said it once, I've said it a million times. Without extensive reading, don't expect great understandings of the practical workings of your psychic tools. Your skills are dormant, and the reading material will be instrumental in awakening your spirit's memory banks. Historical background will enhance your assimilation, as well as provide knowledge of the folklore surrounding this tool.

DEMONS AND DEVICES

In the age we live in, our freedoms have been totally compromised by technology. Indeed, every day that passes adds another link in the chain that technology wraps around our lives like a vise. True, there are great benefits that have been afforded humanity. But within the spirit world, a new, electronic, charlatan has set up shop on the block…

I constantly see the Internet ads luring the public toward psychics that advertise all kinds of little miracles. You will sign in online and the person will "chat" about the problems you put forth. It's an age old practice that has switched stages. Whatever, it still smells of snake oil vendors!

Cell phone deities abound these days. For a simple click you can decide a major dilemma in your life. The phone also has services whereby the so-called psychic reads questions from prepared flyers. These are designed to keep the caller on for a prescribed period of time, after which anything the "psychic" says is fair game as far as the employer goes.

Imagine that. A major decision by the unsuspecting caller left in the hands of a psychic telephone service where neither client nor server see or know each other! The personal vicinity of the aura, the spirits, the vibrations, and emotions of both client and reader are in the vapors. That intimate interaction which charges any reading is substituted by a cold screen or recording. A stranger whose only identity is their "stage name" and voice.

However, even worse than the above in the fraud being committed by pretending to realize rituals through skyping over distances. In the Hispanic community we often joke about doing "santo por fax". In short, it's poking fun at those that fall for these charlatans that sell these rituals online for quite a large amount of money. I've heard and seen how these con artists have the ignorant stand and receive instructions of rituals that they are allegedly receiving while both simultaneously go through the steps that the charlatan dictates. Afterwards, or sometimes even before, the client then sends the money, unless these people have credit card facilities and it's done right then and there. It's sad to think that people believe they are being cleansed or initiated through this conduit.

Yet, the client in these cases is just as much to blame. Often the desire to hide under the cultural radar pushes their arrogance into this. They are apparently oblivious to the fact that their very punishment is the money they spend on these empty relics. I think that if anyone does even the minimal research into the best way to receive a valid reading or any spiritual service, they will be led to reputable places.

Once again, nothing is comparable to experience. Which is why in Latin society we harp so much on word of mouth references. When people relate their actual experiences with a spiritist and what that person was able to help them with, it prepares the future client for a living encounter, full of reality. It is still the best system of reference around. You can give anyone a business card, but when that card is accompanied by personal recommendations based on experiences, then you really have been given more than any commercial advertising could ever provide. Remember this when you look for your readings in the future.

And now—tomorrow...

As I wind this down, I ponder how the spiritist movement will have evolved. My dream is to see the Anglo parlance grow within the temples. I yearn to see many a Mesa Blanca performed totally in English, sticking true to the Kardecian philosophy. As the world becomes smaller and smaller, the day is not far when there will be misas in just about any language.

To all the mediums out there: you are not alone. Don't allow members of religions to be aggressive toward you without a response. We are living in the middle of another Dark Age in this 21st Century. Everywhere you hear the cry for liberty, yet, when you look at what is being proposed, it's more dictatorial than what is being overthrown. Theocracies are coming up in many areas of the world due to people feeling a need to be saved from whatever they see as evil. What often happens, however, is that what is supposed to save them often turns into its own kind of evil.

Secular governments are being cajoled, bribed, and brainwashed into giving too much special treatment to faith-based groups that camouflage themselves as secular charities, but are really commercial ads for their particular faith. If you were to listen to these fire-brand extremist ministers, the Inquisition would be brought back from the dead of history. Continents such as Africa, Asia, and the Americas have long been flashpoints of hatred and social warfare declared by clerics against mediums. In their wake stand ruined lives and shattered families that have had their unity split, all in the name of God. Every religion swears it has a special hold on the Almighty and they pretend to talk on God's behalf.

Such arrogance should be seen for what it is. But too often the psychological fear factors being worked on by these fanatics gives credence to this posture. The fragility of life today contributes to society's quest for a better and reliable existence. Faith, ironically, is being replaced by messianic figures that wish to be viewed as the saviors of our planet.

Mediums need to be wary of the charlatans among the spiritist movement. Due to these living frauds, we pay for them through the suffering we endure via discrimination and hate. There have even been court cases over this issue of religious liberty. It led to the Supreme Court decision whereby the Santeria Church of Babalu-Aye in Hialeah, Florida, won the legal recognition to its rituals of sacrifice as long as it followed set regulations for the edification or disposal of these.

Though Spiritism, unlike Santeria, Voodoo, Sanse, or Palo Mayombe, is not a religion, nonetheless it is as religious a philosophy as it gets. Prayer occupies the major preparation for all misas. Seances that skip or skim over prayer are not related in any way to the Allen Kardec spiritual work.

To be a medium is to be a gift sent to humanity by the Heavens. Guard it well, for it is always envied, feared, and attacked by the ignorant bigotry of those who would appoint themselves as Earth's messiahs. Just as thoughts have wings, mediums can travel on these wings. Rise…and be counted among the points of light…

* * * * * * * *

Parts of this book were dictated by some spirits from my Quadrant. I owe all of my Spiritual Quadrant unending gratitude for all of their protection, knowledge, and light afforded me since my arrival on this material plane. They provided the necessary help for me to continue progressing through the classroom that is life.

I pray that these later years of my existence grant me continued strength to teach tomorrow's mediums how to spread their wings today. When the mentor that is right for you is found, don't treat that relationship lightly. It's as strong as an umbilical cord between the quadrants involved. Don't try to fly alone. Always return to your mentor's nest before you travel further and further. Each return to the nest will provide further knowledge, renewed strength, and wisdom.

A very special prayer of thanks goes out to that pioneer soul of spiritism: Hyppolyte Leon Denizard Rivail, known also by his pen name, Allan Kardec. His grave is still a great attraction at Cimetiere du Pere Lachaise in Paris, France.

In addition, my lifelong gratitude to every medium I've ever shared a misa with and their quadrants. Having experienced sharing the aspects of working with the public, these mediumnistic brothers and sisters have provided strength, loyalty, and all too valuable lessons, both negative and positive, that have contributed to my successful journey.

I leave you with the inscription on Allan Kardec's grave: "To be born, die, again be reborn, and so progress unceasingly, such is the law."

Light unto your spirits…!

NOTES

NOTES

www.ingramcontent.com/pod-product-compliance
Ingram Content Group UK Ltd.
Pitfield, Milton Keynes, MK11 3LW, UK
UKHW022221230426